THE BRONX
Then & Now

Stephen M. Samtur
&
Martin A. Jackson

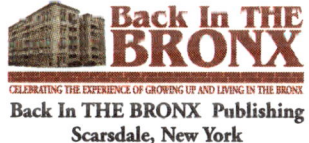

Back In THE BRONX Publishing
Scarsdale, New York

Copyright © 2003 by Back In THE BRONX
www.backinthebronx.com

All rights reserved. No part of this book may be used
or reproduced in any manner whatsoever without written permission.

Typography & Design: Nick Povinelli

Library of Congress Catalog Number 2002116550
ISBN 0-9657221-4-7

Manufactured in the United States of America
FIRST EDITION

Introduction

Cities have a life span, just like people. They are newborn at one point, carved out of forests or deserts, and they pass through adolescence, maturity and (with luck) reach a distinguished old age when they become revered and respected. London, Paris, Rome and New York have passed through these stages of growth and stability, each in its own way, and every other urban center has its own history. If we consider the Bronx a city, and it does have a million and a quarter people, making it a respectable size by any measure, then we can also trace its life story. True, the Bronx is part of an even bigger whole, and it shares in many ways the growth pattern of the larger New York region, but the Bronx has its own special qualities too.

From its founding, or at least settlement, back in the 17th century in the days of old Jonas Bronck himself, to the boom times of the 1920's and 1930's, the Bronx followed its destiny, sometimes in concert with the surrounding city and country, and sometimes going its own way, but always with a distinctive flavor.

In the 20th century, the Bronx traced an interesting and dramatic arc through history. Following its incorporation into the New York City fold in 1897, the Bronx began a period of rapid growth and prosperity. Railroads, subways and roads sprouted magically in the first two decades of the century bringing in business, housing, people, stores and schools, and all the bits and pieces that made the Bronx a fondly remembered place, from Yankee Stadium to the Paradise Theater, along with a few hundred candy stores for a couple of generations.

Growth Brings Problems

It didn't last. The Bronx was, by the 1960's, changing just as rapidly as it had grown; it had reached another stage of growth and just like a teenager becomes an adult, so the Bronx entered another period in its life. This one was not very comfortable for many people and it made the Bronx a synonym for urban problems. Buildings burned, streets got dirtier than ever, schools were troubled and the police talked about "Fort Apache" when discussing the crime situation. A plague of heroin took a chunk out of the Bronx's younger generation in the 1960's and 1970's, and radically altered economic and social conditions changed the borough almost beyond recognition. It was the time when empty buildings were the norm in many parts of the Bronx, and when population decreased at an alarming rate.

But that stage, too, didn't last. In the past twenty or so years, the Bronx has taken giant strides back to health. It isn't the same place that the generation of the 1940s and 1950s remember, but then again, it's a lot better off than it was in the days when Jimmy Carter stood on Charlotte street and surveyed...nothing. On famous Charlotte Street itself, there are rows of attached garden apartments, complete with fences and garages, and little patches of gardens. Along the Concourse, the grand old buildings are cleaner and the trees in good health, and the Paradise is being reopened. Dozens of the notorious empty buildings have been rehabilitated and reoccupied, providing apartments to yet another generation of Bronxites. New companies and new jobs flourish in Hunts Point, while Bathgate Avenue is home to an industrial park, and the Yankees have won the World Series yet again. Problems haven't disappeared, of course. Some streets aren't very inviting, and there are more homeless than necessary, and more asthma too, in the South Bronx. But then, again, the Bronx was never perfect, no matter how we might remember it through the lens of nostalgia.

In this book, we're going to look through that lens at the old Bronx, the Bronx as it was in the early 1940's, and then bring the picture up to date, in the same locations, as it appears today. The comparisons are sometimes amusing, sometimes sad, and always fascinating: it's a trolley ride back fifty years and then a quick return to the present moment and, we hope, with a new perspective on your favorite borough.

Recreation and Relaxation

There are 42 square miles of land that make up the Bronx, with a surprisingly large proportion of that in the form of parks; it is claimed that the Bronx has more park land than any other urban region in America. It surely has the single largest park in New York City, with Pelham Bay Park at more than 3,000 acres taking that title from such patches of green like Central Park and Prospect Park. It can also verify its claim to America's first public golf course, in Van Cortlandt Park, which dates from 1898. All this in a borough whose recent reputation rests on slums, gangs and violence. To those who lived in the Bronx, however, parks were a part of daily life, since nobody lived very far from one. Even in the congested Mott Haven area, St. Mary's Park provided green space and even recreation centers, while farther north and east there were choices galore. Some preferred the wilds of Van Cortlandt, where the land is almost unchanged since the days of Jonas Bronck, while others were drawn to the watery pleasures of Orchard Beach, one of Robert Moses' more useful efforts in the Bronx. The Tremont section had Crotona Park, with its inviting pond for boating and fishing, and world class ball field, while the vast Bronx Park on Pelham Parkway was home to both the Botanical Garden and the Bronx Zoo.

Of course, there were informal parks as well. Every street could be a playground or a football field, and every wall, stoop and lamppost could serve a purpose in one game or another. The developers probably weren't thinking of basketball or "off the point" when they designed their buildings in the Bronx, but creative kids found ways to make use of every brick and flat surface. Stickball was the premier Bronx street game, and it could be played wherever there was some open space and an unguarded broomstick. Add a Spaldeen, and there was an outdoor stadium where games might run from dawn to dusk. For more formal sports, of the professional variety, the Bronx was (and remains) the home of the most famous baseball venue in the nation, Yankee Stadium. With the flags of 26 World Championships flying over the tiered stands, Yankee Stadium has been home to the greats of baseball, from Ruth and Gehrig to Mantle and Jeter. The Bronx Bombers have been the class act of baseball since the stadium opened in 1923, and their pinstripe suits have helped keep the pride of the Bronx alive during some difficult years.

Games were not the primary purpose of Bronx life; at least that's what parents thought. To the grown-ups, school was the place where children belonged, for as long and as often as possible. Luckily, the Board of Education agreed and so created a remarkable network of local schools throughout the Bronx. Coupled with a very active parochial school system run by the Catholic Church, and some other religious groups, Bronx youngsters were destined to spend a sizeable portion of their early years in one school or another. The local elementary school was the first step for most, and it was generally within walking distance of home. "P.S. Whatever" became your alternate universe starting about age 5, when kindergarten was demanded. The schools ran an architectural gamut, from very old 19th century to early 20th, and even a few built in the 1930s and 1940s. Building styles were consistent throughout the Bronx (and throughout New York City for that matter) being products of the centralized Board of Education. There were fake colonial junior highs, pseudo-Gothic elementary schools, high schools in various Classical, Tudor or eclectic patterns, and all under the (usually) benevolent guidance of the principal and staff. Private or faith-based schools like All Hallows, Fordham Prep, or Cardinal Hayes were less standardized and, of course, governed by their church officials in a way that was reportedly far more strict and unforgiving.

The point is that school and the school experience was the unifying factor in most Bronx natives. Attendance until age 16 was required and, for most youngsters, high school graduation was expected. Perhaps not all took the academic program, but whether it was vocational or even general, a diploma was a normal achievement by the 1940's. High school allegiance was very strong for most, who identified themselves as Taft, Clinton, Monroe or Columbus alumni for the rest of their lives. A few might get into Bronx Science, or even travel to Manhattan for such schools as Music and Art, Stuyvesant, or Performing Arts, but these were a minority. For most Bronx dwellers, high school was the district school, and that old jacket with Clinton or Roosevelt on the back is today a precious possession to those with sense enough to keep it. The rest of us have to be content with yearbooks and yellowing pictures, and the occasional high school reunion, to keep the memories vivid.

College became a viable option for many Bronxites,

again thanks to New York City programs. Free education was offered at CCNY, Brooklyn and Queens Colleges, while private schools like NYU and Fordham expanded mightily in the 1950s and 1960s. With time, the system of tuition free higher education grew to encompass community colleges, including, of course, Bronx Community College on the former NYU campus, and even graduate education. By the mid-1960's, thousands of Bronx high school grads had the option of a college education, and many took it. With fiscal disaster in the 1970s, the free tuition rule was dropped, but costs remained modest and drew more and more minorities and disadvantaged young people to the City University system. It was only one of the many new options and movements that shaped the Bronx in the second half of the 20th century.

Immigration and Migration

In the post-World War II years, great change swept over the Bronx. New immigrants arrived in large numbers, replacing the older Jewish, Irish, and Italian communities. The Puerto Rican migration, for example, brought thousands of Spanish speaking newcomers to the South and East Bronx, while a large movement of black people also began to change the demographic identity of the Bronx in the 1950s and 1960s. Added to these were Asian arrivals in the 1960s, Dominicans, Jamaicans, Africans, and Albanians in the 1970s, and immigrants from nearly every nation in the world. The Bronx was suddenly an international settlement, though not all of this went smoothly.

To many of the established communities of the Bronx, these newcomers represented unwelcome change and plunging property values. Already in the late 1940s, the movement to the suburbs had begun and with the help of cheap automobiles, low cost mortgages, and newly built roads, the older white inhabitants of the Bronx began their treks to the new homes in New Jersey, Long Island, and Westchester. Every street and apartment building began to vibrate with the news of another family moving out, and shook their heads over the darker people who were replacing them. To those who had good jobs and better prospects in the boom times of the 1950's, the little house in the suburb was an irresistible lure: "the schools are so much better," it was said, or "the kids can have their own backyard." The great American myth of the frontier still held sway into the 20th century, among Bronxites as well as others, and the lure of green yards, open spaces and a better life out of the city was a powerful draw. Suburban builders and the automobile industry eagerly fed this mythology, resulting in Americans abandoning their urban centers by the millions and putting down stakes amidst the trees and lawns of suburbia. The Bronx was not immune, and those who could saved their money and were finally able to buy their little cottages in Long Island or in Jersey.

For those who lacked the means, a solution was found. In the northeast Bronx, on the site of the former amusement park, FreedomLand, arose the largest co-op project in America: Co-op City. With tall white buildings and carefully planned walkways, parks and open spaces, Co-op City was a marvel of engineering and social planning. When it opened its doors in the mid-1960s, the time was ripe for an exodus of Bronxites who were uneasy about the changing demographics of their neighborhoods, the stories of rising crime, and who longed for a better life. The populations of the West Bronx, Tremont, Pelham, and Fordham were convinced by the sales campaign and put their money down on the clean and "modern" apartments being offered by Co-op City. While there was no overt racial quota, the new inhabitants of Co-op City turned out to be largely Jewish and Italian, and overwhelmingly white. Whole neighborhoods were emptied, as if by magic, and the racial balance of the Bronx tipped dramatically toward the Latin and Black families who gladly occupied the now-empty apartments on Prospect Avenue, or White Plains Road, or on University Heights.

Co-op City was, in its way, a success. It was occupied rapidly and did offer a better living standard for many. But it was one of the markers of the overall change that was ravishing the old Bronx. Equally notable in the changing times of the 1960s was the Cross Bronx Expressway, a monstrous road building project directed by the lordly Robert Moses, which imposed a multi-lane express highway through the heart of the Bronx and further propelled the exodus of the old inhabitants. First proposed in the early 1950s, the Cross Bronx Expressway was touted as a solution to the troubling traffic congestion of the automobile age, providing a rapid passage through the Bronx that linked New England and the rest of America. Trucks and cars would speed along the Expressway on their way to business and the homes of the new suburbs, and everyone would benefit... So proclaimed Moses, and so it was done. The niggling problem, however, was that the road demanded the demolition of hundreds of apartment houses, private homes and small businesses across the Bronx, from the Harlem River all the way to the Triborough Bridge in the East. On paper it made sense; in the real world, it was a death knell for the stable lifestyle that Bronxites had known since the early 1900's, and it represented the triumph of the automobile over the poor and middle class people who had carved a life in the Bronx. In those days, Moses was not to be denied, and the Expressway chewed its way across the borough with only minor obstacles posed by politicians and the people affected. By the early 1960s, the Cross Bronx had become a sunken ribbon of concrete that had torn apart the East Bronx.

There were so many kinds of buildings. The Bronx was, of course, famous for its apartment houses and living spaces, and it still is. The borough is thickly populated with the five- and six-story dwellings that house more than one million citizens, and some of those apartment houses are famous for their design. But the category of Bronx architecture is not limited to living quarters: in the Bronx there are also factories, churches, colleges, museums, public schools and public offices, stores and commercial spaces of every description, as well as the parks, stadiums, beaches and hospitals that form an infrastructure for a bustling city. The traces of every wave of immigration and every school of design can be found in the solid stone and concrete of the Bronx, from the dreary utility of the one-story taxpayer stores to the dazzling facades of the Bronx Zoo and Loew's Paradise. Not so many years ago one could still see the farms and barns of the 19th century, and a few might still survive in the farthest reaches of Pelham or Mott Haven. The sturdy gingerbread of the 19th century lingers in more than a few stores along Tremont Avenue or on the shores of Country Club Road along the Sound.

Unifying the Bronx

In the 19th century, the Bronx was a series of unconnected hamlets and villages, such as Mott Haven, West Farms and Morrisania. Each had its own character and the old pictures show us the result: uneven and unplanned building that included homes for the wealthy, summer retreats, factories and wooden buildings that were home to stores and small businesses. Some structures were outstanding, such as the Hoe Factory in Hunts Point or the Victorian train station on Mott Avenue, but for the most part the Bronx was sparsely utilized and without an overall character. In 1874, much of the South Bronx was incorporated into New York City and a network of rail and trolley lines began to tie the Bronx closer to the great center of Manhattan. With the annexation, parks, such as Crotona, St. Mary's, and Claremont, were carved out of the open spaces, and a greater civic spirit could be observed. This work was redoubled in 1897, when the remaining western portions of the Bronx were officially incorporated into the City as a borough, and urban planning began in earnest. The great symbol of the Bronx's emergence from rural sleepiness was the plan for the Grand Concourse and Boulevard, proposed and championed to completion by the civil servant, Louis Risse. Beginning in the 1890s, Risse argued, fought, and directed the building of this impressive boulevard designed to imitate the great avenues of Europe and to be the artery of Bronx life into the new century. Remarkably, given the nature of New York City politics and real estate, Risse lived to see his boulevard opened and acclaimed as a civic wonder. Running from Mott Haven in the south all the way to Mosholu in the north, the Concourse instantly became the premier address in the Bronx and the showcase for some remarkable architectural advances in the 20th century. Other early and significant building projects include the Bronx Zoo, a world famous institution that has enthralled millions over the years, along with its neighbor, the Bronx Botanical Garden on Fordham Road. Nearby, too, was Fordham University with its Gothic buildings still in use. New York University also took advantage of the open spaces of the Bronx to build its hilltop campus (and the Hall of Fame) on University Heights. The Bronx Municipal Building in Crotona Park (now gone) was a landmark for many decades, while the American Bank Note Building in Hunts Point drew customers worldwide for its printed material, especially currency notes. Still, the Bronx of the 19th century was a relatively undeveloped and sparsely populated place, though change was coming with great speed as the new century dawned.

A Melting Pot of Architecture

The energy of 20th century architecture is visible from Mott Haven to Riverdale, and from Orchard Beach to Highbridge. On the whole, the Bronx is a creation of the 20th century, despite the colorful remnants of earlier years. When the population began to surge around 1900, and grow more rapidly in the 1920s, builders and developers scrambled to provide the housing and offices for these new inhabitants. Luckily, 20th century styles and building technologies provided just the solution for the fast-growing borough with its vast empty fields and new horizons. Unlike Manhattan or Brooklyn, older, more developed boroughs and cities in their own right, the Bronx offered a nearly blank slate to the real estate industry. Experimentation and innovation was, if not encouraged, possible in many cases . . . and sometimes welcomed as a successful selling feature. The pressing need at first was for affordable housing and reliable transportation for the waves of new arrivals from the older sections of the city: Jews from the lower East Side, Irish from Hell's Kitchen, Germans from Yorkville, and Italians from Little Italy. All made their way to the Bronx in the opening decades of the new century and staked their claim to a better life.

There they met the established inhabitants of the Bronx, the old English, Dutch, and German settlers who had come generations before. In addition, there were pockets of African-Americans, especially in Morrisania, and a varied mix of established Americans and immigrants from every part of the world. The opportunities for development were obvious — vigorous demand and limited supply of housing — and the result was a real estate boom. Fortunes were made (and sometimes lost) by trading Bronx properties in the early 20th century as the needs of the newcomers were energetically fulfilled by the more-than-willing builders and brokers. Tenements sprouted magically in Mott Haven, West Farms, Tremont, and Hunts Point, while elegant apartment buildings were built along the Concourse and Pelham Parkway. Without central planning, of course, the outcome was a dizzying mix of new and old, modern and old-fashioned, but with a vigorous spirit that captured the optimism of the times.

The Bronx became the architectural melting pot that captured the energetic mood of the 1920s. Along the Concourse, the new imported style of Art Deco captivated the better-off renters: sharp angles and interesting new designs were in demand for those who could afford the high rents (more than $100 per month) for Concourse dwellings, such as elevators, sunken living rooms, doormen and elegant lobbies, complete with mosaics and marble floors. For the less affluent, the construction industry offered less expensive apartments, but with amenities such as courtyards, ample windows, and "modern" kitchens. For the working class, even the tenements were advertised as being light years ahead of the old slums of Manhattan, with kitchens, private bathrooms, and plenty of sun and air. The formula worked, as thousands of families flocked to the new neighborhoods along Tremont, Fordham, and Pelham in fulfillment of the American Dream. Along with the thousands of new apartments, the city erected schools, parks, playgrounds, and civic amenities that seemed like fantasy after the crowded years in the Manhattan slums.

This was the era when the classic Bronx apartment house took shape. Usually five stories, possibly six, but only with an elevator, the apartment house was a modern answer to the ancient problem of making a city livable for very large numbers of people. In the Bronx of the 1920s and 1930s, the solution was moderately priced rental apartments, built in blocks of 40 or 50, with all the savings of scale and mass production. The typical apartment house (and no landlord would admit to the description of typical nor ever use the word tenement) gave the Bronxite some modern amenities that probably were new to their experience. In a three-room apartment, for instance, there was a "modern" kitchen with a gas stove, a refrigerator, and sink, and with varying degrees of luxury, such as cabinets, linoleum floors, and work space. Many of the older buildings came equipped with dumbwaiters, a now abandoned system of garbage collection in which the superintendent used a rope and pulley to collect waste directly from each apartment . . . it was a special delight for kids to wait for the little elevator to be announced by a bell and to load the trash. The "super" was a central figure, in fact, in Bronx apartment life: he usually lived on premises (often in the basement), took care of sweeping the streets, mopping the halls, and, with luck, was able to fix small emergencies in the water and electrical systems. He was also the undisputed authority for the local kids, and policed such infractions as throwing the ball too close to windows, sitting on the steps, making a mess in front, and creating noise . . . all of these activities, of course, would be reported to parents, with the usual dire results. Many of the newly built apartment houses came with gardens, sometimes quite extensive with statuary and walkways. More common was a small patch of green shrubbery in front, but it was still a garden and another sign of betterment to those who came from the solid concrete and brick of the Manhattan (or European) slum.

Other useful and attractive features of Bronx lifestyle included a carriage room for the expected flood of children, a rooftop drying line for clothes, an awning for the summer sun, and a modicum of decoration in the lobby or entrance. Builders often took the liberty of naming their buildings, so the Bronx is well populated with carved stone inserts proclaiming the "Dolores" or "Lincoln Arms," if not some literary reference, such as "Avon" or "Trilby." For the really large multi-unit projects, there would be a unifying theme, perhaps Tudor, with false wood beams, or Moorish, with some exotic Eastern elements, like tapestries in the lobby or minarets on the corners. A true luxury residence, on the Concourse or a similar upscale street in Riverdale or Pelham, would naturally offer greater swank. Drop living rooms were a perennial favorite in the Bronx, and involved a step or two down onto the polished floor of the living room from the entry foyer, and, in the best addresses, apartments might have two bathrooms and the desirable casement windows. Elevators were, of course, expected in the best buildings, and many may remember having elevator operators, although they weren't standard. But Bronx elevators were pretty widespread by the mid-20th century and, in fact, made possible the increased height of the buildings; fewer people each year were willing to climb four or five flights to their apartments.

However, the comforts of Bronx tenement life should not be exaggerated. These wonders, like elevators and modern kitchens, were unknown in vast stretches of the East and South Bronx, where five-story walk-ups were the standard, and life could be hard. Thousands of apartments were built for working people who commuted every day to jobs in Manhattan, and their lives were only slightly improved from their origins in the old slums of the City. True, there was running water and almost always indoor plumbing and private bathrooms, along with heat and electricity, but the rooms were cramped, and the service was haphazard. Living in Morrisania or Mott Haven, on Courtland Avenue or Kelly Street, was not exactly the "better life" promised in real estate advertising.

Like most big cities in the early 20th century, New York was the result of individual taste and business necessity. Whole neighborhoods sprouted from the farms and empty fields, without any particular guiding principle, and so we had the Bronx as a bewildering mixture of both good and pedestrian design, factory and dwelling, schools and shopping centers. Zoning laws were flexible in the first half of the 20th century, and political influence could override the most troublesome rules; the real estate lobby was inordinately influential in Bronx affairs in the 1920s and 1930s, and few could stand against the argument that growth was paramount and niggling rules were secondary. What emerged finally was a borough that varied wildly from commercial to industrial to residential, with little if any demarcation between the zones. Side by side with expensive residential units were garages, small industries, and municipal offices, along with schools, parks, and electric substations. In the 1930s especially, as the New Deal poured resources into the Bronx, municipal construction changed the shape and nature of the Bronx. Bridges, such as the Triborough, altered the transportation pattern of the city, while parks and open spaces, like Orchard Beach, changed the recreational life of its people. Schools, health centers, playgrounds, and such projects as the Bronx Municipal Market, made their presence felt. It was a Depression, true, but much was accomplished in the Bronx, and much of that still remains.

'The Borough of Universities'

In some quarters, the Bronx is known as "The Borough of Universities," and with some reason. The rambling campus of Fordham University on Rose Hill in the Fordham section dates back to the late 19th century, when the good Jesuits found suitable land in the far-away Bronx and began construction of their Gothic center of learning. It has been expanded and updated with more modern styles of building over the years, but Fordham has remained solidly a Bronx institution after educating several generations of lawyers, doctors, and businessmen. The other major center of learning was New York University, nicely sited overlooking the Harlem River on University Heights in the West Bronx. In a burst of creative energy, the trustees of NYU, which began its life in Greenwich Village (and where it remains today) decided to build a satellite campus in the far north. They chose the hills just south of Fordham Road and commissioned the great architect William Sanford White to design the entire project. He responded with a classic and rigorous plan of Beaux Arts buildings and prepared lawns that reflected early 20th century faith in education and Classical education at that. The great commons is surrounded by Greek revival classrooms and a domed library, so that anyone who entered would understand that he or she was in the presence of great thought. Even more, in keeping with Roosevelt era patriotic fervor, White added a colonnade to the library in which busts of great Americans would be displayed for the public's edification, the acclaimed Hall of Fame.

There were other imposing buildings and municpal structures throughout the Bronx, most taken for granted by the people who passed them daily. Courthouses, schools, statues of war heroes, churches, and grand structures were part of the landscape for millions over the years. Many remain today, such as the towering glass greenhouse in the Bronx Botanical Garden, while others have faded into history. Still others – the Municipal Court Building on Third Avenue, is an example – have fallen into ruin, but may yet be rescued. The architural background to Bronx life was frequently more impressive than we knew, but it was woven into the fabric of those days . . . and remains with all the other details, as part of our memories.

A Note on Picture Postcards

The turn of the 20th century was a time of great excitement and wonder throughout the world. Science, industry, education, and all the arts seemed on the verge of new greatness, and nowhere was this more evident than in New York City. All of America, true, shared this optimistic mood of the early 1900's (think of Teddy Roosevelt as a symbol of the times), but it was New York City that seemed to be the exemplar of the new age. Grand buildings were rising as if by magic, and shiploads of immigrants swelled the city's population to historic heights; nothing, it seemed, was beyond the dreams and reality of Gotham. A small but revealing part of this time of change and vigor was the picture postcard, which has come to represent the technology and underlying social movements of the day in ways which might not have been considered by the early printers and sellers of these humble souvenirs. All over the world, the postcard was the rage: In Japan, they were beautifully designed in traditional motifs, while the great steamships made sure their passengers had free postcards to mail home. In England, picture postcards became part of the vacation experience, especially for the working people who flocked to resorts like Blackpool and loved the slightly bawdy cards they could mail to friends in the factory or pub. French tourists sent back cards from Rome, and Russians mailed pictures of the Pyramids; everybody, it seemed, was on the road and making sure they had plenty of picture postcards.

The many picture postcards we have included in this volume give us only a small taste of the richness of this uniquely 20th century form of communication. We have naturally chosen pictures of the Bronx, and for the most part, they are very early pictures of the parks and monuments that Bronxites thought noteworthy in the 1900's. Postcards of Manhattan are, of course, even more numerous and more widely used. But the very presence of Bronx picture postcards suggests the existence of two things: one, a cheap and efficient technology to manufacture the cards, and, two, a large market for them. Both of these conditions were present in the 1900's, and their story is an interesting one.

What seems to us a very obvious method, that of sending short messages by postcard rather than by long (and expensive) written letters was, in fact, a late invention. Not until the mid-19th century did some American and German innovators suggest using convenient cardboard rectangles for everyday or casual notes, and charging the minimal postage to deliver them. Only the briefest notes could be penned, but for many people, both senders and receivers, that was enough. The prodigious letter writers of the Victorian Age could dash off hundreds of words in their letters to colleagues or family, and it was considered a necessary skill in good society. They did, however, pay richly for this privilege and, in some countries, it was the letter's recipient who paid the postage. Long and heavy correspondence was therefore not a hobby for the common or working class family. Enter the postcard, upon which cousin Emil from Hamburg, or Aunt Effy from Cincinnati, could say hello and report a bit of urgent travel news or the birth of a child, all on the back of a postcard. The convenience and economy of this new format quickly won the public's approval, and, by the 1800's or so, most of the industrialized world, such as Britain, Germany, the U.S., and France had amended their postal laws to permit, and even encourage the postcard. These early cards, though, were strictly utilitarian, with only a minimum of decoration, and hardly ever a picture. People, it seemed, were ready for something more colorful and artistic, and they were soon to be satisfied by the power of modern technology.

Photography had existed since the 1840's and, by the end of the 19th century, several methods had evolved to permit widespread use of the camera and reproduction of the pictures. Photography had become, by 1895, a hobby for the average person with inexpensive cameras and simple darkroom or developing techniques. The explosive success of George Eastman and his Kodak camera ("You take the picture, we do the rest.") proved the appeal of picture-taking by the masses, and soon hardly anyone traveled without the pre-loaded and single-focus Kodak camera to record the scene. Professional photography grew more mature as well, with clumsy and difficult view cameras and traveling darkrooms replaced by sleek and highly evolved camera equipment, so that every event, monument, and moment of importance could be recorded. Picture-taking had become a part of everyday life by the time the 19th century drew to a close. This progress in photography was matched by equally revolutionary progress in the printing arts, notably the development of color lithography in Germany. By using a century-old method (printing from engraved stones) and adding the magic of modern chemistry, optics, and high-speed printing, German factories were able to reproduce huge numbers of pictures, calendars, advertising posters, and any other printed matter in full color. Color was no longer added by hand by skilled craftspeople (often women) and therefore reserved for the well off customer. By 1900, the whirring presses of Germany could pour out nicely colored (even artistic) reproductions by the millions, and so make them available to the mass market. It took only a moment for eager businessmen to realize the potential: use the new print machinery to make cheap picture postcards, and sell them to the already established market around the world. If people liked using bare-bones cards, how much more would they like cards with beautiful color views of the Eiffel Tower, or the Brandenburg Gate, or the tall Municipal Office Building in New York City. For that matter, maybe they would also buy color cards with local scenes: the lake, the hotel, the one-street downtown area, or the new church, so that friends in other regions could enjoy the wonders of every small town and resort. In fact, it had become quite easy to enter the postcard business. German sales representatives toured America (and the rest of the world) offering bargain prices for the printing and delivery of boxes of nice cards, each tailored to the local or business interests. A drug store owner, for example in Kansas City, could become a postcard publisher with the help of a local photographer, the German printing company, and the cooperation of the U.S. Post Office.

The printers and distributors guessed rightly, of course. There was an avid market for picture postcards made up of the newly mobile and relatively prosperous new middle class that had been born during the 19th century. Travel had become a familiar pastime by the 1890's, with events like the Paris Exhibition of 1900 or the Chicago World's Fair in 1896, giving tremendous momentum to the travel industry. People from around America who would have never gone more than a dozen miles from their home towns suddenly were driven to take railroads to big cities and historic sites . . . and they sent picture postcards back home. Buying, selling, sending, and collecting these colorful cards quickly became a passion for thousands around the world (including Queen Victoria of Britain, who established a royal collection), and the numbers produced and mailed soared into the uncountable millions. From Seattle to Boston, every hotel, drug store, museum, railroad stop, or scenic view sprouted a stand selling postcards. No chamber of commerce in the nation would overlook the sale of postcards celebrating its town or city, and it was viewed as poor taste to travel without sending home a few illustrated postcards for family and friends.

And so we return to the Bronx. The energetic real estate dealers of the Bronx had no trouble in seeing the value of good publicity for their borough, with its wealth of pleasant scenery and attractive buildings. Photographers were recruited to take scenes of the new Grand Concourse, or the Botanical Garden and Bronx Zoo, or the Hall of Fame. The photos went to Germany (although American printers made deep inroads into this industry as well) and soon a bundle of pretty postcards would be on sale for pennies at Bronx stores and offices. Many of these views of street scenes were "improved" in the printing phase, so that the grass was greener and the buildings were even more appealing, but this was considered fair artistic license in the 1900's and provoked little concern. The goal was to present the Bronx, newly incorporated into New York City, as a healthy, attractive, and prosperous city where the new arrivals to America would find an urban paradise. Every picture postcard sent back to Poland, Alabama, or London made the Bronx seem a garden spot; and it was a sales campaign that apparently worked very well.

Today, these quaint and collectible pictures of an old Bronx are a glimpse into the past. Some of the old buildings and streets remain, hardly changed, while others have been remodeled out of existence. We can still see Poe Cottage as it was in the World War I years, or glimpse the fine houses along Prospect Avenue when horses were the normal means of transport; there is the Keith Theater on Westchester Avenue as it stood in the 1900's, and, on another card, we see the playgrounds that used to line Van Cortlandt Park on Broadway. We know this isn't the Bronx of the 1940's and 1950's, but it makes a connection to the past that is nice to have.

Tax Assessment Photos

Municipal employees were busily engaged in 1940 and 1941 in taking a picture of every (note: every) structure in New York City. This treasure trove of photographic history is preserved in the Municipal Archives, now on microfilm, and this offers a unique opportunity to see what the old neighborhoods really looked like, not what our faulty memories tell us. In those immediate pre-war years, the LaGuardia administration decided that the city tax rolls weren't accurate any longer; they were based on old maps, fragmentary records, and were full of errors. It meant, in short, that the city wasn't getting its fair share in the form of real estate taxes. Some buildings no longer stood, others had been radically altered, and still others built since the tax rolls were last updated. In these pre-computer days, taxes, like all other city business, were a matter of paper and pencil, and the good memories of bureaucrats. It was the modern solution, then, to use photography to remove any doubt about a building's size, location, and overall value: in the future, the tax collector could look up any address and any structure for a fair assessment.

Such was the theory, at least, and to implement this new method, teams of photographers were dispatched to every borough and every street, with orders to take pictures of record for the city's use. It is hard to say the civic authorities had history in mind when they launched this scheme, but these tax photos have become a primary source, especially for the story of the Bronx. Very few photographers would have thought of trudging the streets, alleys, and factories of the Bronx for the sheer artistic rewards, but, thanks to this tax project, we have those streets forever recorded. Want to see how Fordham Road looked in 1941, or how your own apartment building appears in the same year? It's there, along with every garage, outbuilding, two-family house, and kosher butcher store, all thoughtfully recorded by the City of New York.

Acknowledgments

I would like to thank a number of people who have contributed to this book. A very special thanks to Ken Cobb, the Director of the Municipal Archives in N.Y.C., for his patience and cooperation, and for permitting access to the archives' wonderful photos.

Tom Casey, a Riverdale resident and friend, was particularly helpful for making his vast collection of Bronx postcards available. Many of them date back to the early part of the twentieth century and dramatically offers a unique perspective of how neighborhoods looked back then and the way the matching contemporary pictures compare.

Charlie Kraybill, a subscriber to my magazine, Back In THE BRONX, has created a unique on-line album of movie theaters in the Bronx. He graciously allowed us to use some of his post-theater pictures, helping us bridge the gap of time. To view Charlie's Old Bronx Theatre album, go to http://kraybill.home.mindspring.com.

The contemporary photos were the result of the considerable skill of photographer Linda Harris. Not only did she have to match lighting and angles with buildings that no longer existed, she had to also be aware of vehicular traffic. Oftentimes the authors had to prepare a 'protective barrier' by waving arms and imploring drivers to slow down enabling her to take just the right picture. Thankfully we were able to get all the shots without injury.

Fran Gildea, Anne Bauccio, Dorothy Budica proofed the manuscript and were always helpful answering questions. Mark and Michael Samtur spent countless hours at the Municipal Archives meticulously researching pictures, while Adam Samtur put to good use his journalistic background editing the text.

This is the second Bronx book that Marty Jackson and I co-authored and each time he brings a perspective that only a born and bred Bronxite can offer. Maybe we work so well together because over 50 years ago we both lived just a couple hundred yards from one another and attended the same elementary school (P.S. 26) and Junior High School (P.S. 82).

Finally, this project couldn't begin to come to fruition without the dedication of my talented graphic artist, Nick Povinelli. He struggled and oftentimes agonized over picture placements, captions and positioning and a host of things that I take for granted.

Stephen M. Samtur

West 242nd Street & Broadway looking south

This early 1900's postcard reveals the popularity of the Van Cortlandt Park recreation area. The terminus of the Broadway line close to the border of Yonkers attracted crowds of picnickers, nature lovers and sports-minded city folk who relished the open green spaces of the park (left) and the restaurants and amusement rides. Today, the same subway brings new generations who use the Van Cortlandt spaces for soccer, cricket, football and track events among others.

Third Avenue & East Tremont Avenue looking west

This turn of the century postcard underlines the commercial activity that made Tremont Avenue (and the longest street in the Bronx) a Mecca for shoppers and businessmen. One of the long-lasting businesses is Frank's Sporting Good store on the southeast corner of Park Avenue and East Tremont. The El was removed in the late 1970's, but the vitality of the area remains high.

West 187 Street & Cambreleng looking west

This street in the "Little Italy" of The Bronx contributes towards the spiritual and commercial heart of Belmont. The church at right is Our Lady Of Mount Carmel, where generations of local people were baptized, married, and were buried. The neighborhood has retained its unique character, even if diminished in area. Today, it still draws visitors from around the world, and many former Bronxites continue to come for the Italian specialty food.

East Tremont Avenue & Park Avenue (east)

Again, this turn of the century postcard shows the business artery of east Tremont with the Third Ave El in the distance. Horses still dominated the scene, although the trolley car system was in place and the automobile was looming in the near future. The long-established firm of Shipman's Stationery is visible at left (on postcard) at 447 East Tremont Avenue.

East 149th Street & Third Avenue

Known as the Hub, this congested corner of the Bronx drew shoppers by the thousands to the leading departments stores, such as Hearn's, Crawford, Baumann's, and, in later years, Sach's and Alexander's. The Immaculate Conception Roman Catholic Church located at 378 East 151st Street near Melrose Avenue was a spiritual anchor and remains active today. The El has passed into history, but the area retains an active commercial life and plans are underway for improvements.

Photo Courtesy of the New York City Municipal Archives

East 161st Street & Grand Concourse

From the steps of the Bronx County Courthouse, one can see the imposing scale of the Concourse Plaza Hotel. This once grand palace was home to the New York Yankees, who would stay there during home games, and appreciated the short walk down 161st Street to Yankee Stadium. The Concourse Plaza also hosted every major political event and personality, and was the pinnacle of social success for weddings and other special occasions. Lectures, conventions, and even fencing matches enlivened the Plaza during its heyday.

PHOTO COURTESY OF THE NEW YORK CITY MUNICIPAL ARCHIVES

Bronx County Courthouse

At the intersection of the Concourse and 161st Street stands the linear face of the Bronx County Building, which replaced the earlier Bronx Borough Hall, located at the top of the hill at Third Avenue and Tremont. It was built in the early 1930's. Inside, there are courtrooms, municipal bureaus, and the Bronx Borough President's office. Its radical design caused a small sensation at the time and it remains a notable piece of New York City municipal architecture. This was and still remains a busy traffic and pedestrian intersection.

PHOTO COURTESY OF THE NEW YORK CITY MUNICIPAL ARCHIVES

Grand Concourse & McClellan Street

In the 1940's, 1950's, and 1960's, the "Y" offered courses in Jewish studies, but, to most, it offered a rich social environment for teenage activities, such as co-ed dances, music lesson, crafts, and sports.

PHOTO COURTESY OF THE NEW YORK CITY MUNICIPAL ARCHIVES

East 167th Street & Grand Concourse (east)

There has been little change at this busy intersection since the 1940's. Morrisania Hospital was nearby, along with the 167th Street Cafeteria and the Kent Movie Theatre.

East 161 Street & Gerard Avenue

The changes here are striking. The contemporary buildings are streamlined and McDonald's has replaced Nedick's at the corner of River Avenue. This same block was home to the well-known Addie Vallen's, the Stadium Bar, a busy place during game time and host to many Yankee parties. Bronx men of draft age in the 1940's, 1950's, and 1960's may remember the Selective Service office on Gerard, where one would be required to register for the draft. Receiving a draft card was a rite of passage for 18 year olds.

PHOTO COURTESY OF THE NEW YORK CITY MUNICIPAL ARCHIVES

161 Street & River Avenue

Under the welcome shade of the Woodlawn-Jerome El in 1941, one notices the familiar Nedick's sign promising hotdogs and their special orange drink. By the 1950's, the eatery moved one block north and remained a familiar meeting place before and after games. The Earl Theatre on 161st Street has since become a Coffee Shop.

The Bronx — Then & Now

Photo Courtesy of the New York City Municipal Archives

Elliot Place & Jerome Avenue

In the early 1940's, this was a classic Bronx street corner: a candy store at street level, a bowling and billiard parlor above, a shoe store and bakery for more essential needs. Food is still important, however television and electronics have changed the leisure life of the neighborhood.

Photo Courtesy of the New York City Municipal Archives

170 Street & Jerome Avenue

The entrance and exits for the Woodlawn-Jerome Avenue El were the neighborhood's commercial hub. Often the corner was occupied by a candy store and/or newsstand and small food shops, and restaurants were not far away. For the straphanger, the stores offered egg creams, cigars, cigarettes and the early and late editions of the New York Daily News and Daily Mirror. For some, the racing forms were an essential purchase prior to their Yonkers Raceway excursions. In the 1970's, you'd get a key made at Mel's and your baked goods at the Garden Bakery at 62 E. 170th Street.

PHOTO COURTESY OF THE NEW YORK CITY MUNICIPAL ARCHIVES

Jerome & Marcy Place

Another Bronx candy store occupied this familiar corner spot in the early 1940's. It served the needs of the neighborhood, both young and old alike. In the sixty years since, the more recent Hispanic population has shaped the neighborhood in its image, but the El is still in service, and the same apartment building is occupied by the most recent wave of newcomers to call this area home.

Photo Courtesy of the New York City Municipal Archives

Jerome Avenue between 182nd & 183rd Streets

The Oxford Theater was one of the larger local theaters in the west Bronx. It attracted movie fans from Tremont, Burnside and Fordham neighborhoods in the 1940's and 1950's. Near the El was often the choice location for shop owners. Close proximity to the station was an advantage for the retail merchant. In summer especially, the shade of the El was most welcomed and Bronxites learned to ignore the rumble overhead.

PHOTO COURTESY OF THE NEW YORK CITY MUNICIPAL ARCHIVES

The Fordham Skating Palace

The Fordham Skating Palace was located between 190th and 192nd Streets and Jerome Avenue. It offered professional level roller skating on polished wooden floors, complete with musical accompaniment. It was a prime destination for Saturday night dates and catered to skaters of every age and ability. Couple skating was gently encouraged and more than a few romances started there with a slow skate under the revolving ballroom lights. Today, the building is occupied by Monroe College.

PHOTO COURTESY OF THE NEW YORK CITY MUNICIPAL ARCHIVES

Kingsbridge Road looking east across Jerome Avenue

The old Kingsbridge movie showed second run films, but was a very popular Saturday morning destination for neighborhood kids. Kingsbridge Road was a thriving business and shopping district as well as a crowded Woodlawn-Jerome El station because of its proximity to Walton HS, Hunter College, Kingsbridge Veteran Hospital and the famous Kingsbridge Armory. Plans have been made to redevelop the sight of the empty Armory.

PHOTO COURTESY OF THE NEW YORK CITY MUNICIPAL ARCHIVES

Jerome Avenue and East Mosholu Parkway North

This street between Gun Hill Road and Mosholu Parkway was an active shopping area and also home to several memorable Bronx restaurants. This view shows Schweller's Delicatessen (off to the right), quite possibly one of the most upscale delis in the Bronx, in part because the waiters wore tuxedos. More in line with Bronx budgets were others like Katz's, further north, and Epstein's (formerly Rogers Deli), closer yet to Gun Hill Road, as well as the Mosholu Cafeteria shown in our picture.

PHOTO COURTESY OF THE NEW YORK CITY MUNICIPAL ARCHIVES

East Tremont Avenue & Belmont Avenue

Close to Crotona Park and the old Bronx Municipal Building on Third Avenue, this familiar strip of stores offered everything from toys to Chinese food to home furnishings. The Deluxe Theater was across the street and the Fairmount was a few blocks east.

Photo Courtesy of the New York City Municipal Archives

East Tremont Avenue & Bathgate Avenue

The Number 40 bus carried shoppers across Tremont Avenue and many would have headed towards the Bathgate Avenue Market (south of this intersection). The slightly more affluent might have shopped here for shoes at Tom McAn's and clothing at Baldwin's, or further west at Frank's Sporting goods.

Photo Courtesy of the New York City Municipal Archives

Fordham Road & University Avenue

This intersection is directly opposite St. Nicholas Of Tolentine and across the street from Devoe Park. It was a major bus and trolley intersection for transportation to Orchard Beach, Alexander's, and points east, such as Belmont Avenue restaurants, the Zoo and Botanical Garden. The bucolic Aqueduct just behind the tall apartment building offered a pleasant stroll in warm weather. Today, little has changed at this corner.

Jerome Avenue & Fordham Road

Even back in 1920, Fordham Road was a prosperous center of Bronx commerce. You had a 12-lane bowling alley and billiard hall attesting to the popularity of these sports before the advent of radio, television, and the palatial theaters like the Paradise and the Loew's Grand. Today, traffic occupies center stage and Woodlawn-Jerome IRT has brought many thousands more to this artery.

PHOTO COURTESY OF THE NEW YORK CITY MUNICIPAL ARCHIVES

Fordham Road & Creston Avenue

The familiar two-story design often housed dance studios, real estate and lawyer's offices and were popular as well with dentists and doctors. Alexander's Department Store was a relative newcomer to Fordham Road at this time, but soon became the best-known Bronx department store. In the early 1940's, ping-pong, bowling, and billiards drew enthusiastic players. Today, although Alexander's is gone, Fordham Road still distinguishes itself as the prime shopping area in the Bronx.

Photo Courtesy of the New York City Municipal Archives

Fordham Road & Creston Avenue

Alexander's offered the best bargains. Men could dress from head to toe at Crestford's, while Bush Corsets could fulfill women's special needs. A bewildering array of clothing still lures customers of any age or fashion taste. Alexander's sadly is still available for rent.

Fordham Road & Creston Avenue

In this 1941 photo, it is interesting to note that Alexander's hosted a restaurant and bar called Rosenhann's. This experiment was short-lived and, by the 1950's, this area of the store was converted to additional retail space. Most stores in these pre-air-conditioned days would mount canvass awnings to stay cooler and offer shade for passing shoppers. At the moment, the building is closed and waiting for future redevelopment.

Photo Courtesy of the New York City Municipal Archives

Webster Avenue & Fordham Road

This view reveals the variety of stores available to the shopper of the early 1940's. Campers and vacationers made Greenberg's a vital part of their summer plans and, in the background, the sign for Rogers Department store (later Sears) is prominent. The street still retains a good deal of vitality and specializes in consumer electronics.

Fordham Road and East Kingsbridge

This was a busy prime location for billboards in the early 1940's. *Gone With The Wind* was still playing (probably its second run) and Chesterfield cigarettes were also well promoted. At right is the Indian Walk Shoe Store favored by parents for their quality children shoes. Today, the strip of stores has recently been renovated, suggesting that Fordham Road still offers much for commercial tenants.

East Kingsbridge Road close to Fordham Road

The Windsor Theater was one of the most important and foremost vaudeville locales in the Bronx. Live performers continued to appear throughout the 1940's and some of the bigger stars of the times performed for enthusiastic audiences. In this case, dancer Ray Bolger and a full vaudeville program is appearing. Today, the theater façade has been removed and the Windsor Theater is now a popular dining spot.

Photo Courtesy of the New York City Municipal Archives

Webster toward Fordham Road

Looking south is Rogers Department Store, one of the pioneers in department-store-style selling. By the 1950's, it was bought by Sears Department store and today still remains a solid anchor for their redevelopment program.

The Bronx — Then & Now

3rd Avenue & East 190th Street

This stations stands overhead and a Nedick's occupies the valuable retail location at the corner of Fordham Road. This area was located near Roosevelt High School and Fordham University, as well as the Fordham stop for the New York Central Railroad. Today, the Bronx Redevelopment Program severely altered the appearance of this area.

PHOTO COURTESY OF THE NEW YORK CITY MUNICIPAL ARCHIVES

Theodore Roosevelt High School

This high school is located on Washington Avenue and Fordham Road, and served a wide district in the Belmont-Arthur Avenue area. Some of its prominent graduates are June Alyson, Chazz Palminteri, and Dion DiMucci.

Photo Courtesy of the New York City Municipal Archives

Bathgate Avenue & Fordham Road

Little has changed in the 60 years between these two photos. It is still home to an auto supply store, and it continues to attract billboard advertising.

Photo Courtesy of the New York City Municipal Archives

Fordham Road & Lorillard Avenue

The original White Castle was a great success, thanks to its 5-cent burgers and, perhaps, its choice location next to P.S. 45 and Roosevelt High School. The store is still in business in a larger space in an updated building. In the 1950's, White Castle also drew crowds with its carhop service.

Fordham Road & Crotona Avenue

The 1940 Packard is being advertised at the dealership. This huge Packard showroom stood right angle to Fordham Hospital, Bronx Zoo and adjacent to the Bronx Botanical Garden. Today, a tunnel carries traffic beneath the intersection and the showroom is now a Motor Vehicles Bureau.

East 189th Street between the Grand Concourse Valentine Avenue

As every Krum's fan knew, there was a rear entrance to the delights of the store. While the Fordham Road entry was large and well advertised, this connecting building stood around the corner on East 189th Street and allowed for passage through the lower chocolate store. A few steps up would bring the sweets seeker to the fountain and restaurant level, but many preferred this small private path. The building stands today, Krum's sadly has moved its factory to Pearl River, N.Y.

Fordham Road & Concourse

Back in the late 1920's and early 1930's, this intersection was dramatically different. Apartment buildings surrounded retail stores and traffic was minimal, as the bicycle rider demonstrates. Today, that corner would be too dangerous for bicycles and sometimes even for pedestrians. The familiar Wagner building on the left replaced the original apartment buildings in the late 1930's.

Photo Courtesy of the New York City Municipal Archives

Fordham Road & Concourse

Above the underpass was a popular intersection for crossway pedestrian traffic going to and from Alexander's. It was also the site of the well known Armed Services recruiting station. In 1941, one could see all the way to the top of the Paradise Theater. Today the theater still stands, but is not in use.

Concourse just north of Fordham Road

In the mid 1960's, Sutter's Bakery was still attracting crowds. Not long after this picture was taken a fire gutted this great bakery and today it is the home to a discount store. Many will remember the mocha cream squares and wonderful butter cookies.

Concourse & Fordham Road

Back around 1910, this intersection was quite different. There was a paucity of vehicular traffic. The policeman was directing traffic, though one might ask why. Today, the picture is dramatically different. An underpass now takes vehicular traffic under the Concourse. For more than 50 years, the U.S. Armed Forces Recruiting Center still occupied this location. Most of the apartment buildings had yet to be built.

167 Street & Walton Avenue

The only visible change in this scene seems to be the absence of the trolley and the replacement paving over of the cobblestones. A block away (west) was Morrisania Hospital and Loew's 167th Street movie theatre.

The Bronx — Then & Now

Morris Avenue & East 167th Street

This important intersection connected several trolley lines (note the power lines above). There was the familiar Bronx vista of corner candy stores and food shops along the avenue. On Morris Avenue, a taxi stand awaits passengers. The names of the stores have changed, but Jordan L Mott Junior High School stands nearby.

The Bronx   Then & Now

PHOTO COURTESY OF THE NEW YORK CITY MUNICIPAL ARCHIVES

College Avenue & East 167th Street

This apartment building, a bold venture in design, still stands. Air-conditioners replaced old-fashioned awnings. What was a vacant lot in the early 1940's is now Jordan L. Mott Junior High School.

Teller Avenue & East 167th Street

A classic candy store occupies this corner spot. Cars are few and far between in the 1940's, but 167th Street is supplied with a crosstown trolley. The street is basically unchanged today, but the candy store is gone.

The Daughters Of Jacob Home

The Home still stands at 167th Street and Findlay Ave. The palatial estate still retains its elegance and sense of security and continues to care for the elderly from the surrounding area. It's apparent that the well-cared-for trees have grown vigorously in six decades.

East 165th Street & Sherman Avenue

In the 1940's, this intersections could accommodate any necessity. You could find a drug store, a deli, a bakery, shoe repair shop, bar and grill, and a mini food market. In recent times, supermarkets replaced smaller stores.

East 165th Street & Walton Avenue

This intersection hasn't drastically changed in more than 50 years. The new style street light and the smooth asphalt pavement identify this modern picture. Otherwise, the neighborhood remains stable.

Jerome Avenue & Shakespeare Avenue

At the foot of Highbridge is a typical mix of stores, traffic, and pedestrians on a brisk day in the Bronx back in the 1940's. The density of population in this area, combined with its hilly nature, necessitated a more compact shopping district. Hence, the number of stores you see here on Jerome Avenue. Today's population is similar in size and has similar needs.

East 167th Street & Jerome Avenue

If you lived in this area, you probably used the Number 35 bus as your crosstown connection, especially if you wished to travel to the far end of the east Bronx or to 181st Street and Broadway in Manhattan. In the more recent photo, fast-foods seems to have replaced furs, buses replaced trolleys, and the new lampposts create a more cluttered appearance.

East 169th Street & Sheridan Avenue

Fedoras were worn in the 1940's and Jacob Rupert's Bronx Brewery was still supplying neighborhoods. Parking rules seemed unnecessary in those times, and alternate side parking was unimagined back then.

Photo Courtesy of the New York City Municipal Archives

Sheridan Avenue & McClellan Street

P.S. 90 is just out of picture, but the stanchion is directing traffic away from the intersection. These portable-rolling stanchions would be moved before and after school hours for vehicular traffic. The replacement of zebra stripes crosswalk seem a feeble attempt to regulate traffic today at this same intersection.

Photo Courtesy of the New York City Municipal Archives

West 170th Street & Cromwell Avenue

Those living in the Highbridge section of the Bronx would recognize this familiar intersection if they rode the Number 11 bus after getting off the Woodlawn-Jerome train station at 170th Street. For those looking for part-time employment, this area housed several taxi garages. The building has remained intact and now serves as the Highbridge Community Life Center.

PHOTO COURTESY OF THE NEW YORK CITY MUNICIPAL ARCHIVES

City Island & Bridge Street

If you had five cents in 1941 and could get to it, you could buy a jumble-malt or a frank and sauerkraut, or a frozen custard at the famous Nickel Palace. The only problem was that you probably would have had to make the long trek to City Island. Next door, one sees evidence of City Island's maritime interest. Modern City Island is a major attraction for the tourist and New Yorker alike, both of whom flock there for seafood and fresh salt air.

City Island & Marine Street

This charming 19th century house has been transformed from a restaurant to a private residence over the years. The widow's walk on the roof in 1941 is gone and the porch has been removed, but the basic structure is intact.

Photo Courtesy of the New York City Municipal Archives

East 187th Street & Crescent Avenue

Here is one of the streets in the heart of Belmont. People would meet outdoors, shop for specialty items, and catch up on the latest gossip. Italian was heard more than English on the streets, and by the 1950's, restaurants and retailers had learned about the benefits of conversing in English and attracting tourists to the area. Today, streets seem emptier and less exciting, although Belmont is a leading destination for visitors to New York.

East 187th Street & Hughes Avenue

A pharmacy has stood on this corner for at least 60 years. In 1941, it was called Pharmacia Italiana and obviously catered to the many Italians living here. Since 1950, the Amato Pharmacy has continued the tradition of serving the neighborhood's medical and pharmaceutical needs.

Longfellow and Home Street

This dreary street scene reflects the hard times that affected many in the late 1930's and early 1940's. It was always a poor and working class district and the Depression took its toll here. Sixty years later, hard times seem to linger, although car ownership is more widespread.

PHOTO COURTESY OF THE NEW YORK CITY MUNICIPAL ARCHIVES

Southern Boulevard & Westchester Avenue

Back in 1941, this corner drew crowds of shoppers and EL riders. The elegant apartment building housed the familiar Manufacturers Bank and six decades later another bank. The New York National Bank occupies the same site. There has been little change to the building over the years, and the intersection is still the scene of vibrant activity.

Westchester Avenue & Southern Boulevard

Looking north in the early in the early 1940's, you could get hamburgers, frankfurters or root beer for a nickel, which served the daily needs of the straphangers coming from and going to work. Today, this location serves a different population. The frankfurters and hamburgers are long gone, replaced by a pharmacy and health center.

Westchester Avenue & Rogers Street

This was home to an elaborate Russian & Turkish Bath House for both men and women. The large numbers of east European immigrants savored the old custom of steaming, followed by a plunge into a cold water pool. In the 1940's, the building became the elegant Tropicana Club, where Cuban cuisine and Latin music were served up three or four nights a week, with floor shows and first-rate dance bands. Today, the structure is on the verge of renovation.

PHOTO COURTESY OF THE NEW YORK CITY MUNICIPAL ARCHIVES

Prospect Avenue between East 161st & East 163rd Streets looking north

Woolworth and the RKO Franklin movie theater occupied a prominent space on this busy and even upscale stretch on Prospect Avenue. People arrived by bus, train, and trolley to shop and to be entertained. The Franklin was one of the premier theaters in the Bronx. Today, much has changed and there has been an obvious effort at urban renewal.

Prospect Avenue between East 163rd & East 165th Street

The Loew's Burland Theater located at 164th Street is visible and the inviting display of fruits and vegetable at right would also appeal to pedestrians. In the early forties, before the giant supermarket chains arrived, Bronx shoppers had a wide choice of such local stores. The view is less inviting today, although rebuilding efforts continue.

West Tremont Avenue & University Avenue

At this graceful intersection, where West Tremont meets University Avenue, a bewildering variety of stores serve the area residents well. Across the street, on the east side of University Avenue, was the Park Plaza Theater and P.S. 82. It was the center for school and social life. The trolley tracts are gone, and the stores are different, but the neighborhood continues to thrive.

Photo Courtesy of the New York City Municipal Archives

Featherbed Lane & Nelson Avenue

In the 1940's, a bank was incorporated into the large apartment building on Nelson Avenue, perhaps because of the street's proximity to the Featherbed Lane business district, as well as University Avenue. Three wings of the building seems to have survived the years well.

The Bronx · Then & Now

Photo Courtesy of the New York City Municipal Archives

Featherbed Lane & Macombs Road

Featherbed Lane seemed to have ample traffic in 1941 as we look west towards University Avenue from Macombs Road suggesting a lively shopping street. Today, the same view reveals even more traffic, and in the distance one could see the Sedqwick Housing Project built in the 1950's.

Edward L. Grant & Nelson Avenue

This area serviced part of the Highbridge community close to the Harlem River. The hilly terrain made transportation a chore and people relied on the trolley system to get them to their subway stop. Manhattan commuters would have to travel to Jerome Avenue elevated line at 170th or even further to the IND subway on the Concourse and 170th Street or even across the bridge at 181st Street and into Manhattan for the A train. The cobblestones on Edward L. Grant are gone, as are some of the buildings in this view.

Morris Avenue & East 161st Street

161st Street is a major east-west thoroughfare, with Yankee Stadium located at the western end. A large municipal building is located on the southwest corner of Morris Avenue and today has been joined by even more city offices, court, and police buildings. The street has now become a center of government activity and has been extensively rebuilt.

Teller Avenue & East 161st Street

This formidable building appears to have survived and even improved over the sixty years since the photo. Commuter trains still travel nearby on Park Ave. Throughout the 1950's, the nearby popular steakhouse *Alex & Henrys* drew a loyal following, including many New York Yankees players.

Photo Courtesy of the New York City Municipal Archives

Third Avenue, Melrose, & East 149th Street

Bronxites knew this area as 'The Hub' in 1941 and it still retains that name today, despite the changes in Bronx life over the years. The El is gone and so is Nedick's and stores such as Alexander's and Sachs have passed into history, but the crowds still come for bargains.

Photo Courtesy of the New York City Municipal Archives

Third Avenue & East 152nd Street

In 1941, the original Alexander's store was in its infancy and, within a decade, opened its more famous store on Fordham Road and the Concourse. This bargain store in 'The Hub' lured generations of Bronx shoppers. The site is now occupied by similar retailers, selling inexpensive clothing for the whole family.

PHOTO COURTESY OF THE NEW YORK CITY MUNICIPAL ARCHIVES

Third Avenue & East 150th Street

Old timers will remember the Sachs Furniture Store jingle with its familiar telephone number, MELROSE 5-5300. A favorite place for home furnishings, Sachs was one of the mainstays of 'The Hub' shopping district and prided itself on the high quality of its merchandise. The old store has been replaced by a similar business, but today shopping is done without the rumbling of the El overhead.

Morris Avenue between East 169th Street & East 170th Street

In 1941, the synagogue was called Talmud Torah Sons of Israel and offered extensive services to this largely Jewish community. Aside from worship, there was a day school and a catering hall for weddings and Bar Mitzvahs. Today, it remains a religious institution, although it serves a different faith and is called Church of Christ.

Findlay Avenue & East 170th Street

The store changed its name and new populations arrived, but this solid looking building continues its original function, providing modest housing for working people. Claremont Park, across the street, offered greenery and recreation to several generations of neighborhood children.

Teller Avenue & East 170th Street

The ground floor of this building was occupied by a local Democratic club and they actively supported the re-election of Franklin D. Roosevelt to an unprecedented third term as President of the United States. Among the heavily Democratic Bronx voters, Roosevelt was practically unopposed in what became four successful campaigns for the nation's highest office. Today, the apartment building has been razed and the space occupied by a used car lot.

The High Bridge

The graceful arches of the High Bridge seen from Sedgwick Avenue and West 167th Street still serve their original function into the 21st century. In reality, an aqueduct rather than a bridge, the High Bridge carries water from as far away as the Catskills into Manhattan.

The High Bridge

The High Bridge originally permitted pedestrian traffic, and strollers took advantage of the beautiful view of the Harlem River Valley. The bridge was opened in the mid-19th century and is one of the oldest municipal structures in the Bronx.

Ogden Avenue & Merriam Avenue

The design of P.S. 11 is typical of a late 19th century school and was repeated throughout the five boroughs, although very few still exist. After more than a century of use, the school recently was replaced by the modern building in our picture. The school continues to serve the Highbridge community.

White Plains Road & Lydig Avenue

In 1941, Marilyn's Dress Shop on the corner of Lydig Avenue seems to have succeeded at this location and perhaps allowed local ladies to avoid the long and arduous trip to Manhattan to buy a stylish dress. The stores today appear to be equally prosperous and varied as they continue to serve the community of Pelham Parkway. The elevated train continues to provide access to the rest of the borough and beyond.

Cruger Avenue & Lydig Avenue

This was clearly a popular and busy corner for the Pelham Parkway neighborhood in the early 1940's. The Palace Deli occupied the prime location on the corner, and later moved a few feet west, where it stood for a few decades at the corner of Lydig and White Plains Road. It remained a prime attraction for teenagers well into the 1960's. In today's photo, the same corner and its adjoining stores still provide every possible service to local residents.

Bronx Parkway North & Pelham Parkway North

This classic piece of art deco was a powerful lure to well off tenants in the early 1940's and helped make this part of Pelham Parkway an elegant address. The building has been remarkably well maintained. The only apparent change is the corner window replacement, possibly to accommodate modern air-conditioning needs.

Westchester Avenue & Union Avenue

This dreary looking building was a bank in the 1940's in this working class neighborhood in the east Bronx. Local merchants and manufacturers found it convenient. Today, the bank is gone and the building stands empty.

Westchester Avenue & Prospect Avenue

Prospect Avenue was a major shopping venue in the east Bronx, with several movies nearby and a convenient Prospect Avenue elevated station. Once home to many wealthy residents, Prospect Avenue had become middle class by the 1940's. The London Hat Shop on the corner suggests that fashion was still considered important in this middle class neighborhood. Hats have passed out of favor, most of the movies have closed, but the neighborhood, after the turbulence of 1970's and 1980's, is being revitalized.

Lafayette Avenue & Hunts Point Avenue

Cobblestones and trolley tracks are a prominent reminder of an older Bronx and the light traffic and wealth of parking spaces also remind us of another time. Far left once stood Hunt Point Hospital until the mid-1940's and in the newer picture, the site is now an empty lot.

Photo Courtesy of the New York City Municipal Archives

Lafayette Avenue & Manida Street

Buildings such as these on Lafayette and Manida in the Hunt Point section are an example of the building boom of the 1920's. In the background is P.S. 48 on Spofford Avenue, one of the elementary schools so critical to the stability of the neighborhood. Nearby is the Rodman L Drake Park.

Photo Courtesy of the New York City Municipal Archives

Hoe Street & Westchester Avenue

These modest buildings located near the Westchester Avenue and Southern Boulevard transportation hub reveal the high population density in this industrial area. Jobs were found in nearby Hunt's Point or via easy access to Manhattan. The corner candy store provided amenities in a neighborhood where there were few. The buildings today have been repaired and preserved and offer housing to yet another generation of hard working people.

Bryant Avenue & Westchester Avenue

A trolley car makes its way past three impressive apartment buildings in the early 1940's. The streets are oddly free of auto traffic, but private autos in those days weren't routine. Many walked, or used the public transportation system to connect to the rest of the city. In the contemporary view, these solid structures have weathered the years well.

White Plains Road & East 222nd Street

Sides of buildings back in the 1940's were often in demand for advertising. In this case, Eichler's Beer, has a prominent spot on White Plains Road and was one of the many small beer producers in the Bronx. Eichler's is long gone but advertising continues in the same location.

East 149th Street & Morris Avenue

In 1941, Crawford's Clothes advertised men's suits for $19.95 on their large sign high above 149th Street. This major east-west thoroughfare connected the Bronx to Manhattan and was the pathway to 'The Hub.' The buildings have only slightly changed, although the neighborhood has seen some dramatic building in recent years, including the huge Lincoln Hospital. Joey's Hero Shop on the left has been serving sandwiches for more than half a century.

Castle Hill Avenue & Bruckner Boulevard

The restaurant Joe & Joe occupies the site that dates to the mid-19th century when it was Bailer's Hotel. It has been Joe & Joe since 1940 and, in modern times, has expanded to occupy the former billiard parlor next door.

Washington Avenue & East 176th Street

The Bronx Winter Garden at 1874 Washington Avenue was the venue for live entertainment, political meetings, and sporting events. Named after the original Winter Garden in Manhattan, this decorative building was a successful effort to uplift the cultural life of the Bronx dating back to the 1920's. Today, the building is intact, although with a different purpose.

Photo Courtesy of the New York City Municipal Archives

White Plains Rd. & Gleason Avenue

Aside from the graffiti in the modern picture, this corner still serves as a local meeting place. Single or attached housing was the rule in this neighborhood. For more sophisticated shopping, Parkchester offered larger stores, such as Macy's.

East 133rd Street & Lincoln Avenue

At the tip of the Bronx, in the heart of the old Motthaven District, the Ruppert Brewery was one of the larger beer makers in the city. Colonel Jacob Ruppert was the driving force behind the building of Yankee Stadium in 1923 and a longtime owner of the team.

Bruckner Boulevard & Lincoln Avenue

This imposing industrial building housed one of several piano factories, making the Bronx an unlikely center of piano production. The close proximity to the East River made shipping easy and may have accounted for its success. The building is now being refurbished for loft housing, and the entire area is undergoing a striking renaissance.

East 161st Street & Morris Avenue

Some private houses and high-rise buildings offer a contrast in style and time periods in this contemporary photo. Even in 1941, the street already had mixed character. The familiar taxpayer building on the corner was topped by some colorful billboards.

University Avenue & Fordham Road

Looking north on University at Fordham Road in the early 1920's already reveals a densely populated neighborhood with trolley cars being the prime means of transportation. Devoe Park is at left and not far on Fordham Road is the imposing St. Nicholas of Tolentine Church. In the more recent photo, one can see Kingsbridge Veteran Hospital.

East 187th Street & Arthur Avenue

This is the center of The Bronx's 'Little Italy' and a powerful lure for tourists who relished the home cooked meals at the local restaurants. Back in the 1940's and still today, one could find the Roosevelt (currently Ann & Tony's), Dominick's and Mario's, just to name a few.

Southern Boulevard & East 175th Street

Southern Boulevard in the early part of the 20th century was a fashionable and flower-decorated thoroughfare, popular for strolling and shopping. Decades later, there is still an effort to beautify the street, although many of the buildings have been razed.

Third Avenue & East 149th Street

The great shopping center known as 'The Hub' in the years around World War I drew shoppers by train and even by horse-drawn carriage. Automobiles were, however, a rarity in those years. Today's Hub is packed with buses and cars, and the El is gone, but shoppers still come in large numbers.

Boston Road & East 168th Street
These buildings date from the early 1900's and even then the neighborhood was densely occupied. What is striking about the two pictures is how little this view has changed in a century.

Prospect Avenue & East 162nd Street

In this early 20th century view, wagons were horse drawn and automobiles hardly existed. The El was, however, already built, and Prospect Avenue was preparing for a more rapid period of growth. The grass mall unfortunately has not survived and the Burland and Prospect theaters have also disappeared.

East 149th Street & Third Avenue

The elevated train disappeared in the mid-1970's and its absence is striking in these two views. The street advertising is still aggressive today, but the old signs are perhaps more charming. The street as a whole has not lost its vitality over the decades.

East 149th Street & Prospect Avenue

The old and new views of Prospect Avenue looking west are oddly similar, considering nearly a century has passed. With the exception of the trolley cars seen in the early view, and new street lighting and new paving, a visitor from the past would feel at home. The school at the right is still at the same location.

PHOTO COURTESY OF THE NEW YORK CITY MUNICIPAL ARCHIVES

Concourse & East 159th Street

The Bronx Municipal Building at East 161st Street speaks of authority and competence in its design and commanding presence over the Grand Concourse. Built in 1931, this structure is home to the borough president and scores of municipal offices and courts. On the west side of the Concourse is Franz Sigel Park.

East Tremont Avenue & Webster Avenue

In the 1900's, this gentle slope was known as Mt. Hope. Nearby is the more familiar Mt. Hope Place and Echo Park. The school in the older picture still stands, although it is now hidden by apartment buildings.

Southern Boulevard from 149th St., Bronx, New York City.

Southern Boulevard & East 149th Street

Looking south on Southern Boulevard is Samuel Gompers High School, a structure that didn't exist when the earlier picture was taken. Southern Boulevard has a small town look, with tall trees and a wide boulevard with hardly any vehicular traffic.

East 149th Street & Third Avenue

A horse drawn cab waits for customers, and pedestrians stroll placidly across the wide street of 149th Street and Third Avenue. Casual strolling is no longer possible at this major intersection of 'The Hub' and horses, along with the elevated subway, are a thing of the past.

204th Street, Looking West from Webster Avenue, Bronx, N. Y.

East 204th Street & Webster Avenue

Today, this part of the Bronx is in the Norwood section and is a largely residential area as this busy shopping street looking west on 204th Street would suggest. In the decades after World War II, many Irish immigrants found homes in this area, contributing to its Irish character.

McKinley Square

Located at 167th Street and Boston Road, this was once a great crosstown trolley hub. The earlier picture suggests a vibrant town where woman used parasols on their way to Fays Department Store. The small park continues to offer a pastoral waiting spot: back then for trolleys, now for buses.

Boston Road & Jackson Avenue

At the confluence of Jackson Avenue and Boston Road stood a sizeable city health center which seemed to draw mothers and children to the dentist and other health-related services. The five-story tenements on Boston Road were built well enough to survive into this new century without much visible change. Automobile styles, however, are radically different.

Washington Bridge

Today, at University Avenue above the Cross Bronx Expressway stands the busy Washington Bridge linking Manhattan and the Bronx. The earlier picture portrays a quieter time in Bronx history. In earlier days, lampposts were a work of art. To some, the bridge was known as the University Avenue Bridge. Pedestrians would often walk across this span on balmy summer evenings.

161st Street & River Avenue

This picture show some of the changes that have shaped Yankee Stadium in the last 50 years. Looking toward the left field foul pole from River Avenue, a notable structural change is visible. The bleachers have been heightened and the old grandstand supports have been strengthened and modernized. The Stadium was renovated in the 1970's.

155th Street Viaduct

At the turn of the century, this steel bridge between Manhattan and The Bronx attracted strollers with baby carriages for an afternoon walk. The view over the Harlem River was peaceful and only horses competed for space on the bridge. In our own day, the vista is considerably less attractive and few would care to push a baby carriage in this vicinity. Nevertheless, the bridge still brings fans to and from Yankee games.

Claremont Parkway & Third Avenue

Here we see a bird's eye view of Claremont Parkway in 1944 looking west, and apparently taken from the Claremont Parkway Station on Third Avenue El. Bathgate Avenue shoppers spilled out onto Claremont Parkway with their bargains, while others may have drifted east for a Sunday picnic in nearby Crotona Park.

East 189th Street & Concourse

In the early 1940's, Krum's was a thriving business and drew chocolate lovers and hungry shoppers from Fordham Road. Both Alexander's and the Paradise Theater were within walking distance. Alexander's is no longer there, and Krum's candy factory has relocated to Pearl River, N.Y., and is doing well as a mail order distributor.

161st Street Underpass

The underpass at 161st Street carries traffic beneath the Concourse and crosstown. The trolley emerging is marked 'X' for crosstown, and the sign above directs passengers to IND line. In both pictures, the Concourse Plaza Hotel is in the background. Trolleys disappeared by the late 1940's, replaced by crosstown buses

PHOTO COURTESY OF THE NEW YORK CITY MUNICIPAL ARCHIVES

Gerard Avenue & East 161st Street

Looking east from Gerard Avenue, the Concourse Plaza towers over the Grand Concourse and a familiar assortment of stores line 161st Street, including an appetizing store, a candy store and a hardware store. In the 1950's and 1960's, many passed this corner on their way to sign up with the Selective Service Board.

Fulton Avenue & East 170th Street

Looking north towards the trees in Crotona Park, both in 1943 and nearly 60 years later, the buildings have hardly changed. The absence of cars in 1943 gives the illusion of a wider street than today's crowded and double parking vista.

White Plains Square

At the turn of the century this intersection was actually called White Plains Avenue Square. The elevated line hadn't extended this far north, giving the square a quiet, small town look. In the newer photo with cars and overhead trains, the serenity of a quieter time is long gone. Additionally, housing projects have replaced the wooden frame homes of the past.

Then & Now
Movie Theaters

Art
1077 Southern Boulevard
Built around 1928 with 600 seats.
Now a church.

Photo Courtesy of the New York City Municipal Archives

Photo Courtesy of Charlie Kraybill

Loew's Boulevard
1024 Southern Boulevard
Opened 1912 with 2,187 seats.
Now a church.

PHOTO COURTESY OF THE NEW YORK CITY MUNICIPAL ARCHIVES

PHOTO COURTESY OF CHARLIE KRAYBILL

Boro
752 Melrose Avenue
Built around 1911 with 559 seats.
Now houses a defunct auto repair shop and vacant retail space.

Photo Courtesy of the New York City Municipal Archives

Photo Courtesy of Charlie Kraybill

Bronx Opera House
436 East 149th Street
Built in 1912 with 1,920 seats.
Now a church.

Bronx
438 East 149th Street
The Bronx Theater featured vaudeville and plays
and offered Bronxites an alternative to Broadway.

Burland
985 Prospect Avenue
Opened in 1916 with 1,896 seats., the building now houses a supermarket.

Photo Courtesy of the New York City Municipal Archives

Photo Courtesy of the New York City Municipal Archives

Photo Courtesy of Charlie Kraybill

Loew's Burnside
East Burnside & Walton Avenues
Opened in 1926 with 2,219 seats.
Now a drugstore.

Casino / Willis
250 Willis Avenue
Opened 1923 with seating for 2,166.
Now a supermarket.

PHOTO COURTESY OF THE NEW YORK CITY MUNICIPAL ARCHIVES

PHOTO COURTESY OF CHARLIE KRAYBILL

RKO Chester
Boston Road & East Tremont Avenue
Opened in 1927 with 2,743 seats.
Now vacant.

PHOTO COURTESY OF THE NEW YORK CITY MUNICIPAL ARCHIVES

PHOTO COURTESY OF CHARLIE KRAYBILL

Concourse
209 East Fordham Road
Opened 1927 with 2,430 seats.
Now retail stores.

Photo Courtesy of the New York City Municipal Archives

Photo Courtesy of Charlie Kraybill

Crotona
453 East Tremont Avenue
Opened 1910 with 2,210 seats.
Now a matress store.

Dale
189 West 231st Street
Opened in the 1930s.
Now serves retail merchants.

Decatur

Webster Avenue & East 196th Street

What is today P.S. 54 was once the site of the fondly remembered Decatur Theater.
This local movie house catered to the Kingsbridge-Bedford Park neighborhood.

Photo Courtesy of the New York City Municipal Archives

Photo Courtesy of Charlie Kraybill

Devon / Trend
241 East Tremont Avenue
Opened 1930 with 600 seats.
Now stores.

Dover
1723 Boston Road
Built in 1930.
Now a church.

Earl
58 E. 161st Street
Built 1936.
Now a cofeeshop.

Elsmere

1926 Crotona Parkway
Built in 1914, originally with 1,552 seats, later expanded to 1,721.
Now vacant and deteriorating.

The Bronx · Then & Now

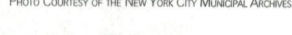

Fairmount

708 E. Tremont Avenue
Built in 1928 with 2,518 seats.
Now a supermarket.

The Bronx — Then & Now

Fleetwood

1000 Morris Avenue
Built in 1925 with seating for 1,650.
Now for sale.

The Bronx   Then & Now

RKO Fordham

Fordham Road & Valentine Avenue

Gone are the RKO Fordham and the smaller Concourse Theater.
The replacement retail shops now make the Amalgamated Bank and clock visible.

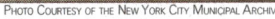

Forum

490 East 138th Street
Build around 1921 with 2,447 seats.
Now a church.

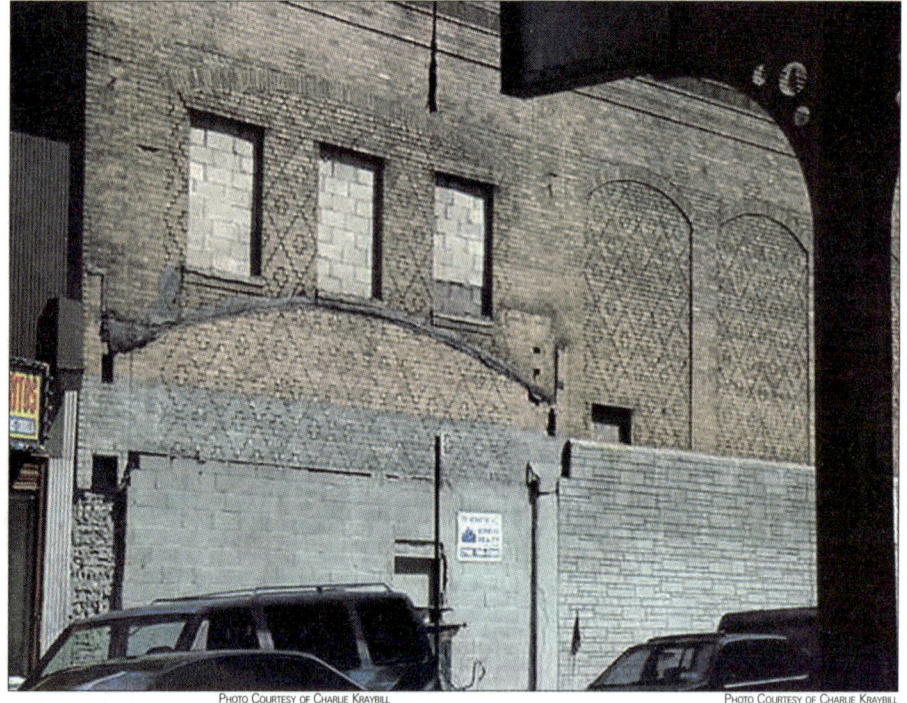

Freeman

1240 Southern Boulevard
Built in 1921 with 1,604 seats.
Now in disuse.

Photo Courtesy of the New York City Municipal Archives

Photo Courtesy of Charlie Kraybill

Loew's Grand
5 West Fordham Road
Built in 1927 with 2,430 seats.
Now stores.

The Bronx — 155 — Then & Now

Photo Courtesy of Charlie Kraybill   Photo Courtesy of Charlie Kraybill

Kent
190 East 167th Street
Built in the 1920's.
Now a store.

Photo Courtesy of the New York City Municipal Archives

Photo Courtesy of Charlie Kraybill

Kingsbridge
15 East Kingsbridge Road
Built in 1921 with seating for 1,125.
Now a supermarket.

Photo Courtesy of Charlie Kraybill

Luxor
15 East Kingsbridge Road
Built in 1921 with 1,125 seats.
Now a supermarket.

The Bronx — Then & Now

RKO Marble Hill
5625 Broadway
Opened in 1927 with 1,638 seats.
Now retail stores.

McKinley Square
1315 Boston Road
Built around 1916 with 1,800 seats.
Now empty and crumbling.

Photo Courtesy of the New York City Municipal Archives

Photo Courtesy of Charlie Kraybill

Mosholu
268 East 204th Street
Built in 1925 with 911 seats.
Now retail space.

Ogden
1431 Ogden Aveue
Opened in 1922 with 1,370 seats.
Now a church.

Oxford
2256 Jerome Avenue
Built in 1928 with 1,950 seats.
Now vacant.

Loew's Paradise

Grand Concourse & East 187th Street
Built in 1929 with 3,884 seats, later increased to 4,100 seats.
Now awaiting restoration.

Park Plaza

1746 University Avenue
Built in 1926 with 2,000 seats.
Now retail stores and a pizzeria.

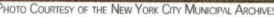

Prospect
851 Prospect Avenue
Built in 1910 with 1,600 seats
Now the Olympic Theater Concert Hall

The Bronx 166 Then & Now

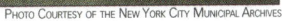

Royal
1350 Southern Boulevard
Built in 1917 with 600 seats.
Now an auto repair shop.

Raymond
City Island Avenue & Reville Street
Now an IGA Supermarket.

The Bronx — Then & Now

Photo Courtesy of the New York City Municipal Archives

Savoy
2341 Hughes Avenue
Also known as Cinelli's and 'The Dumps.'
Now the Enrico Fermi Cultural Center.

Photo Courtesy of the New York City Municipal Archives

Photo Courtesy of Charlie Kraybill

Photo Courtesy of Charlie Kraybill

RKO Spooner
Southern Boulevard & East 163rd Street
Now retail.

The Bronx — 170 — Then & Now

PHOTO COURTESY OF CHARLIE KRAYBILL

Surrey
66 East Mt. Eden Avenue
Built in 1935.
Now a church.

Crescent / Tower
1165 Boston Road
Built in 1914 with 1,693 seats.
Now a church.

Tremont
1942 Webster Avenue
Built around 1910 with 987 seats.
Now a church.

Tuxedo / David Marcus
3464 Jerome Avenue
Built in 1927 with 1,716 seats.
Now retail space.

PHOTO COURTESY OF THE NEW YORK CITY MUNICIPAL ARCHIVES

PHOTO COURTESY OF CHARLIE KRAYBILL

PHOTO COURTESY OF CHARLIE KRAYBILL

Valentine
237 E. Fordham Road
Built in 1920 with 1,252 seats.
Now retail stores.

Photo Courtesy of the New York City Municipal Archives

Photo Courtesy of Charlie Kraybill

Photo Courtesy of Charlie Kraybill

Windsor
315 East Kingsbridge Road
Built around 1920 with 1,600 seats.
Now a restaurant.